Duncan

by Murray Ogilvie

GW00655891

Lang**Syne**
PUBLISHING
WRITING *to* REMEMBER

Lang**Syne**

PUBLISHING

WRITING *to* REMEMBER

79 Main Street, Newtongrange,
Midlothian EH22 4NA
Tel: 0131 344 0414
E-mail: info@lang-syne.co.uk
www.langsyneshop.co.uk

Design by Dorothy Meikle
Printed by Printwell Ltd
© Lang Syne Publishers Ltd 2024

ISBN 978-1-85217-283-1

Duncan

SEPTS OF CLAN DUNCAN OR ROBERTSON:

Collier
Colyear
Donachie
Duncan
Duncanson
Dunnachie
Inches
MacConachie
Macinroy
MacDonachie
MacRobbie
Maclagan
MacRobert
Reid
Roy
Stark
Tonnochy

Duncan

MOTTO:
Disce Pati.

CREST:
Ship under full sail.

TERRITORY:
Angus.

Chapter one:

The origins of the clan system

by Rennie McOwan

The original Scottish clans of the Highlands and the great families of the Lowlands and Borders were gatherings of families, relatives, allies and neighbours for mutual protection against rivals or invaders.

Scotland experienced invasion from the Vikings, the Romans and English armies from the south. The Norman invasion of what is now England also had an influence on land-holding in Scotland. Some of these invaders stayed on and in time became 'Scottish'.

The word clan derives from the Gaelic language term 'clann', meaning children, and it was first used many centuries ago as communities were formed around tribal lands in glens and mountain fastnesses.

The format of clans changed over the centuries, but at its best the chief and his family held the land on behalf of all, like trustees, and the ordinary clansmen and women believed they had a blood relationship with the founder of their clan.

There were two way duties and obligations. An inadequate chief could be deposed and replaced by someone of greater ability.

Clan people had an immense pride in race. Their relationship with the chief was like adult children to a father and they had a real dignity.

The concept of clanship is very old and a more feudal notion of authority gradually crept in.

Pictland, for instance, was divided into seven principalities ruled by feudal leaders who were the strongest and most charismatic leaders of their particular groups.

By the sixth century the 'British' kingdoms of Strathclyde, Lothian and Celtic Dalriada (Argyll) had emerged and Scotland, as one nation, began to take shape in the time of King Kenneth MacAlpin.

Some chiefs claimed descent from

ancient kings which may not have been accurate in every case.

By the twelfth and thirteenth centuries the clans and families were more strongly brought under the central control of Scottish monarchs.

Lands were awarded and administered more and more under royal favour, yet the power of the area clan chiefs was still very great.

The long wars to ensure Scotland's independence against the expansionist ideas of English monarchs extended the influence of some clans and reduced the lands of others.

Those who supported Scotland's greatest king, Robert the Bruce, were awarded the territories of the families who had opposed his claim to the Scottish throne.

In the Scottish Borders country – the notorious Debatable Lands – the great families built up a ferocious reputation for providing warlike men accustomed to raiding into England and occasionally fighting one another.

Chiefs had the power to dispense justice and to confiscate lands and clan warfare produced a society where martial virtues – courage, hardiness, tenacity – were greatly admired.

Gradually the relationship between the clans and the Crown became strained as Scottish monarchs became more orientated to life in the Lowlands and, on occasion, towards England.

The Highland clans spoke a different language, Gaelic, whereas the language of Lowland Scotland and the court was Scots and in more modern times, English.

Highlanders dressed differently, had different customs, and their wild mountain land sometimes seemed almost foreign to people living in the Lowlands.

It must be emphasised that Gaelic culture was very rich and story-telling, poetry, piping, the clarsach (harp) and other music all flourished and were greatly respected.

Highland culture was different from other parts of Scotland but it was not inferior or less sophisticated.

Central Government, whether in London or Edinburgh, sometimes saw the Gaelic clans as

"The spirit of the clan means much to thousands of people"

a challenge to their authority and some sent expeditions into the Highlands and west to crush the power of the Lords of the Isles.

Nevertheless, when the eighteenth century Jacobite Risings came along the cause of the Stuarts was mainly supported by Highland clans.

The word Jacobite comes from the Latin for James – Jacobus. The Jacobites wanted to restore the exiled Stuarts to the throne of Britain.

The monarchies of Scotland and England became one in 1603 when King James VI of Scotland (1st of England) gained the English throne after Queen Elizabeth died.

The Union of Parliaments of Scotland and England, the Treaty of Union, took place in 1707.

Some Highland clans, of course, and Lowland families opposed the Jacobites and supported the incoming Hanoverians.

After the Jacobite cause finally went down at Culloden in 1746 a kind of ethnic cleansing took place. The power of the chiefs was curtailed. Tartan and the pipes were banned in law.

Many emigrated, some because they

wanted to, some because they were evicted by force. In addition, many Highlanders left for the cities of the south to seek work.

Many of the clan lands became home to sheep and deer shooting estates.

But the warlike traditions of the clans and the great Lowland and Border families lived on, with their descendants fighting bravely for freedom in two world wars.

Remember the men from whence you came, says the Gaelic proverb, and to that could be added the role of many heroic women.

The spirit of the clan, of having roots, whether Highland or Lowland, means much to thousands of people.

Chapter two:

Rule of the Duncans

If one family were born to be Scotland's Royal family, it was this one.

When King Duncan I ascended the throne in 1034, he could trace his royal lineage straight back to the country's first ruler, King MacAlpine who by uniting the Scots and the Picts in the middle of the ninth century became known as the founder of Scotland. And outwith a few short interruptions, Duncan's descendants would rule Scotland and England for the best part of the next seven centuries.

But to fully appreciate the immense role the Duncans played in the early history of Scotland and England we must go back through the mists of time past King MacAlpine to the days of St Columba. He was an Irish priest who settled on the Inner Hebridean island of Iona in the year 563. He is credited with spreading Christianity throughout Scotland.

When he died in 597 some of his relics were taken to Ireland and the rest were buried on Iona. Just over 300 years later, when the Vikings invaded Iona, St Columba's relics on the island were taken for safekeeping to Dunkeld by his kinfolk.

The Abbott of Dunkeld was a hereditary position passed through a family which claimed to be among the kin of St Columba. That family are the Duncans. Now in those days family names were not so prominently used, but first names were. And certainly there is a record of Abbot Duncan of Dunkeld being killed after a battle in 965. He is described as Archpriest of the Kindred of St. Columba who claimed descent from Irish royalty.

His son Crinan succeeded him as the Abbot. And he maintained the family tradition of safeguarding the relics of St Columba. When the Vikings attacked Dunkeld in 1045 Abbot Crinnan removed St Columba's bones, which had been kept in the Cathedral, to a hidden destination.

Some years prior to the sacking of Dunkeld Scotland was ruled by King Malcolm II, who reigned from 1005 to 1034 and was head of the House of Atholl. Abbott Crinan married the oldest of the king's three daughters, Bethoc (Beatrice). And their son became King Duncan I of Scotland. By marrying Bethoc, Crinan had aligned himself with Scotland's premier family. Malcolm II was the last king to descend directly through the male line from King MacAlpine.

Malcolm died in 1034 and was buried with his forefathers in Iona. He had no sons so Duncan, his grandson by his oldest child, succeeded him to the throne. Duncan was already a king at this point. Some 16 years earlier, on the death of Owen the Bald, Malcolm used his power and influence to install his grandson as King of Strathclyde. By succeeding Malcolm, Duncan became the first ruler of a united Scotland. Being also the son and hereditary heir of Abbot Crinan, Duncan became Scotland's first Priest-King.

The reign of King Duncan I was short, just over five years. And although in the annals of Scotland it wasn't a particularly important time, it became one of the most-talked about periods of our history, even to this day. And that's down to William Shakespeare.

Duncan was killed by Macbeth, of that there is no doubt. But the circumstances surrounding the plot have been muddied thanks to the English playwright's prose.

There are four completely different versions of how Duncan met his end.

The first is the Shakespearean tragedy. The bard wrote that Macbeth, along with his close friend Banquo, was heading home to Moray after a battle when they were confronted by three witches who addressed him as the Thane (landowner) of Cawdor. They also told him that he would soon be king. The problem for Macbeth is that he was not the Thane of Cawdor. However, just at that moment a messenger from King Duncan arrives. He tells Macbeth that he has just been awarded a new title - The Thane of Cawdor! Coincidentally, a short time later Duncan decided to visit Macbeth in his Inverness castle. Lady Macbeth, deciding that the witches' prophecy is about to come true, hatches a plan to slay the king and put her husband on the throne. At first Macbeth refuses to entertain such a horrific idea. But his evil wife perseveres and persuades him. That night Duncan's guards are drugged into a deep sleep and Macbeth enters the king's bedroom and plunges a dagger into his heart. Duncan's guards are then framed for the murder and killed by Macbeth in a fit of rage.

It made for great reading and acting. But according to historians, almost none of it is true! Yet those same historians cannot agree on what really happened.

Judge for yourself which of the three following 'historically accurate' scenarios sounds the most convincing.

The first describes Duncan as good-natured and easy-going. However, in the Highlands a chieftain by the name of McDowall was leading a murderous insurrection. Duncan was slow to react and before long the north of Scotland was in great turmoil. Duncan, worried that the rest of the country could follow suit and rise against him, sent forces to stamp out the rebellion but they were massacred. At that point Macbeth, who had a great reputation as a warrior, offered to take care of McDowall and his men. Duncan agreed and Macbeth headed north and restored order. Macbeth, who already had a low opinion of the king, is now basking in the glory of victory and begins to covet the throne. Spurred on by his ambitious wife he goads Duncan into a battle. Duncan falls for the bait and in September 1040 near Elgin he leads his forces against Macbeth and is killed.

The second scenario closely resembles the first. Macbeth believes he should be the rightful king of Scotland and is furious that Duncan got there ahead of him. What really infuriates Macbeth and many other Scots is that Duncan is a poor military campaigner. In his time Duncan fought three major battles and all ended disastrously for him. His first fighting foray takes place soon after he is crowned when he decides to go after the Vikings of Orkney. His ships sink en route and he nearly drowns. Next he tries to take on the Vikings again, this time in Ross-shire. But his forces are decimated and he barely escapes with his life. His last, and perhaps most embarrassing defeat comes at the hands of the English in 1039. Duncan and a huge army march south and put Durham under siege in an attempt to conquer Northumberland. But those trapped in the town were able to inflict major casualties on their attackers who ended up retreating in disarray to lick their wounds. By now Duncan's reputation was at rock bottom and Macbeth, realising that the balance of power had shifted away from the increasingly unpopular king, started a rebellion in the north. Macbeth knew that Duncan would have no option but to try and crush him in battle in order to maintain his authority. He also knew that he had a superior force. And so it proved. Duncan attacked Macbeth at Elgin and was slain.

The final scenario is completely different. After the death of King Malcolm II. King Duncan and his cousin Thorfin, Earl of Orkney and Caithness, fell out big time. Duncan wanted Thorfin to give him control of Caithness. Naturally Thorfin refused and the two went to war. After several skirmishes the two armies faced each other in Moray, which at that point was controlled by Macbeth, who also happened to be King Duncan's leading general. When the final battle got underway it became clear to Macbeth that Thorfin possessed the military superiority so he quickly switched sides and ended up with the winners. The spoils of victory were then divided between them with Macbeth becoming the new king and Thorfin retaining his sovereignty in the far north.

Whichever story you believe, two things are abundantly clear. There was much more murder and mayhem to follow involving the Duncans and when the dust settled they were back on the throne of Scotland – a position they were to occupy for a very long time indeed.

Chapter three:

Conspiracy and murder

Duncan's sons, Malcolm and Donald, were very young when their father died and were whisked away to safety because it was thought Macbeth may slay them too. It's thought Donald fled to the western isles, while Malcolm was welcomed in England, which was ruled by Edward the Confessor, who had been exiled himself, and had great sympathy for the young Scottish prince.

It took about 14 years for Malcolm to reach manhood. During that time Scotland under Macbeth was generally peaceful and prosperous. But that was about to change. Duncan's heirs were determined to claim back their father's throne.

Siward, the Earl of Northumberland, was related to Malcolm's mother and would do everything in his vast power to help his young relative. In 1054 Siward, with Malcolm by his side, invaded Scotland at the head of a vast army.

The assault advanced by land and sea and although they inflicted huge casualties on the Scots, Macbeth escaped unharmed. However, the expedition was partially successful. Although Macbeth was still in charge of most of Scotland, Malcolm was left in control of Cumbria and the Lothians.

At this stage Macbeth, who'd earned the reputation as a good king, started to self destruct. Over the next three years paranoia crept in and he began to believe that everyone, including his closest allies, were conspiring against him. Some were murdered while others fled, losing their lands and possessions. Consequently many noblemen began calling for the return of the House of Duncan to the throne.

One of the most powerful, Macduff, the Thane of Fife, sought sanctuary with Malcolm in England. He told the young prince that Scotland was tired of Macbeth and that the time was right to reclaim his inheritance. It was good advice. When Malcolm, aided by Tostig, the new Earl of Northumberland, invaded Scotland the people rallied to his support and many deserted from Macbeth's army to join his. Despite that, there was much fighting to be done before Macbeth was finally cornered at Lumphanan in Mar on August 15, 1057.

It was a popular victory and the people rejoiced ten days later as Malcom known as Malcolm Canmore (great head) was crowned king of Scotland at Scone. Ironically, Macbeth was afforded a royal burial, alongside the king he murdered, in Iona.

In 1066 William of Normandy conquered England and Edgar Aetheling, who should have succeeded to the English crown but was too young, fled to exile in Scotland with his mother and sisters. They were regally entertained by King Malcolm at his royal palace in Dunfermline. One of Edgar's sisters, Margaret, attracted Malcolm's eye and before long the couple were married.

Malcolm carried out several vicious raids on northern England in an attempt to extend his kingdom and although he won the odd battle he always lost the war and was forced to retreat empty-handed.

Margaret, meanwhile, became one of the

best-loved Scots queens of all time. She dedicated her life to religion and to making Scotland a more civilised place. She introduced spiced meat and wine from France along with richly-coloured clothes, dancing and poetry. She taught priests to live piously and turned Sunday into a day of worship. She built churches and gave generously to the poor. She convinced her husband to give to charity and spent many hours in prayer. She also established the Queen's Ferry across the Forth to enable pilgrims to reach the shrine of St Andrew.

Malcolm continued to battle with the English and in November 1093, 36 years into his reign, he and his eldest son, Edward, were killed in a battle near Alnwick. Margaret was critically ill when she heard the bad news and died shortly afterwards. The King and Queen were buried together in Dunfermline Abbey and in 1250, after many reported miracles at her burial site, she was canonised by Pope Innocent IV and became Scotland's first royal saint.

With their deaths the Duncan dynasty really began to spread its wings.

Malcolm and Margaret had eight children. The youngest, Ethelred, died young. The oldest, Edward, died with his dad. Little is known about the second son, Edmund. The two daughters married exceptionally well. Matilda to King Henry I of England, making her queen of England. Their second daughter, Mary, married Eustace, Count of Boulogne, and their daughter also became Queen of England, as the wife of King Stephen.

But it is their three sons who really excelled on the Royal stage. Edgar, Alexander and David succeeded each other on the Scottish throne.

They didn't get there immediately, though. Other members of their family, including their step-brother Duncan II, battled and jockeyed for the crown between 1093-97 when Edgar took over. He was followed ten years later by Alexander, who reigned for 17 years.

But it was the direct descendants of the third brother, King David I (1124-53), who kept the crown in the family for hundreds of years.

The line which was the most influential in terms of Britain's history flowed through his grandson, also David. His great, great, great grandson was Robert the Bruce, who led Scotland from 1306-29. His son, David II succeeded him to the throne and held it for 42 years.

When he died Robert II, the son of Robert the Bruce's daughter, Marjorie, took over. That was 1371 and from then on Scotland's ruling family became known as the House of Stewart. Marjorie Bruce, Robert's only child by his first marriage, married Walter Stewart, 6th High Steward of Scotland. She died in 1316, near Paisley, after being thrown from her horse while heavily pregnant, but the child survived. He was Robert II of Scotland, who succeeded David II and founded the Stewart dynasty.

The Stewart Kings, all direct descendants of Robert II, reigned over Scotland for 288 uninterrupted years. During that time they also managed, thanks to King James VI to take over the English crown as well.

The House of Stewart lost its power temporarily between 1649-60, when Oliver Cromwell deposed King Charles I. But they were back in control with Charles II (1660-85) and his relatives remained on the throne until 1714 when the House of Hanover took over. The German line rules to this day.

There is one final twist to the story of the Duncan dynasty. Despite being Scotland's royal family there is no surviving Clan Duncan. However, their name lives on through a different clan.

By the 15th century, when James I was on the Scottish throne, family names were in common use. The Duncans and their relatives the Duncansons were to be found in large numbers throughout central and south-east Scotland.

In 1437 James I was murdered. One of his followers, Robert Ruabh Duncanson, tracked down and captured the killers and was handsomely rewarded by the Crown. In honour of that great act, his relatives and descendants named themselves "Robert's sons". Through the ages that has been simplified to Robertson. Which is why, to this day, the members of the Clan Robertson are proud to call themselves "Donnachaidhs" – the "Children of Duncan".

Chapter four:

Famous Duncans

The name Duncan has Irish roots and means Brown Warrior. And there are certainly many examples of Duncans with battling qualities living up to their name.

The most famous is Adam Duncan, 1st Viscount Camperdown (1731-1804). As Commander in Chief of the North Sea, Admiral Duncan took on the Dutch fleet just off the village of Camperdown and destroyed it in October 1797. Until that point the Dutch had high hopes of invading England. His victory is regarded by many as the most important sea battle ever won by Britain.

Duncan was born at Lundie, Angus on July 1, 1731. His father was a merchant and Provost of Dundee.

After his triumph he was awarded an annual pension of £2,000 and was created Baron Duncan of Lundie and Viscount Duncan of Camperdown. Along with it came the land which is now Camperdown Park in Dundee. In addition, the pension would pass to his next two heirs. It was the most generous pension pay-out by the British Government to that date. Duncan was also given the freedom of a number of cities, including Dundee and London. Despite all this, however, there was disquiet about the level of the reward, with many believing it was too little. His aunt, Lady Mary Duncan, wrote to the authorities complaining that he should have been made an earl, which is a higher-ranking honour. But the protest fell on deaf ears and when he died suddenly aged 73, at Cornhill, in the Borders in August 1804 he was still a lowly viscount. However, in 1831, his oldest son was made an earl, and his other children, four daughters and a second son, were granted the rank and priveleges of the children of an earl. The Earl of Camperdown built the magnificent mansion in the centre of what is now Camperdown Park in Dundee.

Several ships have been named HMS *Duncan* after him, And in Leeds Duncan Street was also named in his honour. A statue of Duncan was erected in 1997 in Dundee, on the corner of High Street and Commercial Street. In 1999 the Admiral Duncan, a pub named after him in Soho, London, hit the headlines when a nailbomb went off killing three people and injuring over 100. It was part of a bombing campaign against local black and asian communities. The pub, like the war hero it was named after, shrugged off the attack, was rebuilt and continued to thrive.

Another fighting Duncan was The Rev Henry Duncan (1774-1846). He battled on behalf of the poor. Rev Duncan established the world's first savings bank. His investors, mainly local landowners, were paid interest and the profits were used to help the poor in the community. He was born in Lochcrutton, near Dumfries, and was a true son of the manse, with both his father and grandfather being ministers. In 1799, as a graduate, he was offered three ministries by the Church of Scotland. He chose Ruthwell, on the Solway, even though it was the poorest community. In 1810 he founded Scotland's first savings bank. It was so successful that within a few years his bank had been copied all over the UK. He was so determined to make it work that he went to London at his own expense to argue for the introduction of laws which protect depositors. He also founded two newspapers, the *Dumfries and Galloway Courier* and the *Dumfries and Galloway Standard*. The latter is still in existence today.

John Duncan who was born in Kirkcudbright in 1804 was another warrior. He came from farming stock and his strength and height led him to a military career, when he joined the Life Guards at the age of 20. In 1841 he joined HMS Albert on an expedition up the River Niger. More than half of those on board lost their lives but Duncan survived. The experience didn't put him off returning to Africa and three years later he went off on his own to find the Kong Mountains, sponsored by the Royal Geographical Society. It was a highly-dangerous expedition and it became even more worrying when he crossed the path of King Gezo, of Dahomey, who was infamous for his cruelty. However the king was impressed by the brave Scottish explorer and guaranteed his safety.

Duncan failed to find the Kong Mountains but he was one of the first Europeans to explore that part of West Africa. Back home in 1846 he published a book detailing his experiences but he was not fully accepted by the Establishment and his exploits were never truly recognised. Three years later he was back in Dahomey, this time working for the British government. He was now vice consul and was tasked with using his friendship with King Gezo to secure the king's signature to an anti-slavery treaty. He died before completing his task and his bravery and tenacity was later overshadowed by the likes of David Livingston and Henry Morton Stanley.

In recent times, perhaps the most notorious Duncan was Helen Duncan, who was the last person in Britain to be tried as a witch. Ms Duncan, from Edinburgh, was found guilty in 1944 under the 1735 Witchcraft Act and jailed for nine months for pretending to raise the spirits of the dead. Her crime? Putting on séances for relatives of those who died in the second world war. In 2006 she was given a special mention during a ceremony which remembered 81 people from the Prestonpans area who were convicted and killed in the Witchcraft trials of the 16th and 17th centuries.

Ms Duncan had many famous clients, including Winston Churchill, who described the case against her as "Obsolete tomfoolery".

Even though he repealed the Witchcraft Act in 1951, when Prime Minister, a séance held by her in Nottingham five years later was raided by police. It's claimed she died as police officers arrested her while she was in trance.